Percy
the Pink

Written and illustrated by
Colin West

WALKER BOOKS
AND SUBSIDIARIES
LONDON • BOSTON • SYDNEY

Chapter One

There was once a king called Percy.

He had a
pink crown,

a pink tunic,

a pink
cloak

and big
pink
boots.

He lived in the middle of his
kingdom in a castle which was
painted bright pink.

Percy's
place

You see, King Percy loved all things
pink!

He had pink flamingos in the royal
fountains and grew pink carnations
in the royal greenhouse.

ROYAL MENU

BREAKFAST
Pink blancmange
Strawberry milkshake

LUNCH
Pink blancmange
Strawberry milkshake

SUPPER
Pink blancmange
Strawberry milk

And for breakfast, lunch and supper
King Percy ate pink blancmange and
drank pink strawberry milkshakes.

No wonder, then, he was known throughout his kingdom as "Percy the Pink".

Chapter Two

One day, Percy the Pink stood on his highest tower and looked out at his kingdom. It was a wonderful kingdom, but King Percy wasn't happy.

Suddenly he had an idea.

So the king passed a law and had posters put up in the countryside and in the town...

The people weren't pleased. Not everyone liked pink as much as King Percy.

But they learned to live with their new pink clothes.

King Percy looked out over his kingdom.
But he was still unhappy.

He decided to pass another law,
and had notices put up:

Everyone hated this new law just as much as the first one.

But they were loyal subjects and they
painted their buildings bright pink.

Chapter Three

Percy the Pink looked out over his
kingdom. It was better, he thought,
but he was still unhappy.

So he passed another law...

The farmers were far from pleased.
But a law is a law, and has to be obeyed.

Soon every cow,

chicken

and pig

was coloured bright pink.

Once again, Percy the Pink looked out over his kingdom. But he was still unhappy.

King Percy heaved a heavy sigh.

So he passed yet another law and had notices nailed to every tree...

A special pink army sprayed every tree,
flower and blade of grass bright pink.

Meanwhile, King Percy typed a letter to every landlord:

Dear sir or madam,
        You must touch up your home if the pink is peeling off.
        Or else...
                signed
                King Percy

And he sent a reminder ...

Don't forget - all new-born lambs, calves, chicks etc. must be coloured pink in accordance with the law.
Signed
King Percy

N.E. Farmer
Nonesuch Farm
Pinkville

to every farmer.

Flaming Percy the Pink!

29

Chapter Four

Now, you might think that with everything in his kingdom bright pink, King Percy was a happy man.

But heavens above, NO!
For when he looked at the heavens
above, he could see they were still
far from pink!

The King sat down and thought.

Now Eric was the King's Wise Man.
He lived in a cave on a faraway island.

So the King
wrote a note.

Then he gave it to his favourite pink pigeon ...

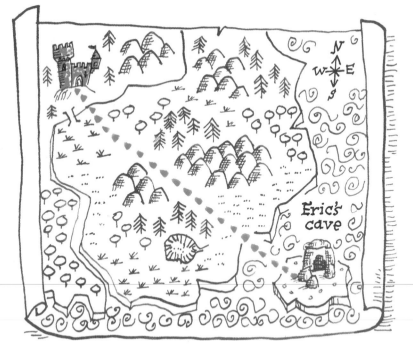

who took three hours to deliver it.

The Wise Man dropped everything
and left for the castle ...

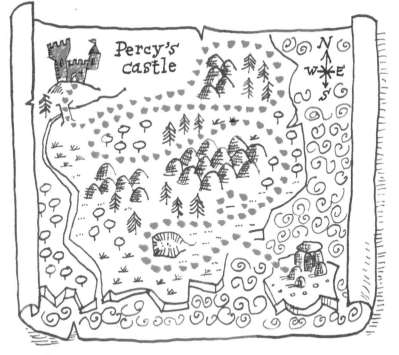

and took three weeks to arrive.

By now King Percy was desperate.
He explained the problem:

Eric was totally stumped.

He had helped the king in the past ...

but this time he didn't know where to start.

But Eric wasn't a Wise Man for nothing. After a week in a special Think Tank, he came up with a brilliant idea.

He found two pieces of rose-tinted glass ...

and he made a pair of glasses.

Chapter Five

The next morning, Eric told the king he had cast a magic spell, which was just beginning to work.

The clouds are already turning pink!

He suggested Percy should wear
a pair of glasses to see things better.
King Percy grabbed them and perched
them on his nose.

He raced to the top of his tower,
and this is what he saw:

(That's right, nothing but pure pinkness!)

King Percy clapped his hands and jumped for joy.

Soon everyone was as joyful as King Percy. They didn't need to dress in pink any more.

And the pink soon wore off their houses and animals.

The trees shed their pink leaves
and new flowers and grass grew.

And soon, everything looked
just as it had before.

But with those rose-tinted glasses,
King Percy was always in the pink!

Walker Starters

The Dragon Test by June Crebbin, illustrated by Polly Dunbar
0-7445-9018-3

Hal the Highwayman by June Crebbin, illustrated by Polly Dunbar
0-7445-9019-1

Cup Run by Martin Waddell, illustrated by Russell Ayto
0-7445-9026-4

Going Up! by Martin Waddell, illustrated by Russell Ayto
0-7445-9027-2

Big Wig by Colin West
0-7445-9017-5

Percy the Pink by Colin West
0-7445-9054-X

Series consultant: Jill Bennett, author of
Learning to Read with Picture Books

First published 2003 by
Walker Books Ltd
87 Vauxhall Walk
London SE11 5HJ

10 9 8 7 6 5 4 3 2

This book has been typeset in
Alpha Normal, Calligraph 810 BT,
Helvetica, M Garamond and
Sanvito Multiple Master

Handlettering by Colin West

Printed in Hong Kong

British Library Cataloguing in Publication Data:
a catalogue record for this book is available
from the British Library

ISBN 0-7445-9054-X